SERVANTHOOD
MISSIONS TRAINING
LEADER'S MANUAL
DON JEFFREYS

WestBow Press books may be ordered through booksellers or by contacting:

WestBow Press
A Division of Thomas Nelson & Zondervan
1663 Liberty Drive
Bloomington, IN 47403
www.westbowpress.com
1 (866) 928-1240

ISBN: 978-1-9736-7087-2 (sc)
ISBN: 978-1-9736-7088-9 (e)

Library of Congress Control Number: 2019910926

Print information available on the last page.

WestBow Press rev. date: 5/13/2020

WESTBOW
PRESS®
A DIVISION OF THOMAS NELSON
& ZONDERVAN

Foreword

According to a 2018 study conducted by the Barna Group and the Seed Company (*Translating the Great Commission),* 51 percent of churchgoers do not know the term "Great Commission." This is a staggering number. The study was very revealing as well as troubling. A decline in Great Commission education within local churches over the last several decades has produced believers who have a limited understanding of biblical missions. Such a decline has also produced believers who do not understand the panoramic view of God's self-revelation from eternity past to eternity future as well as not understanding their place in God's redemptive story. We are now dealing with, and have dealt with in the recent past, the results of a lack of proper biblical teaching on the Great Commission. There are specific examples of such Great Commission education taking place, but it is rather isolated while the majority of churches do not emphasize or provide such basic biblical discipleship. Such a reality is evidenced in the findings of the 2018 study.

As our churches engage with an ever-changing culture, we need practical training manuals, which assist us to meet the challenges we face. *Servanthood* seeks to reverse the downward spiral of biblical ignorance and preparedness our churches are experiencing. The materials you are about to study will assist you and you church as active participants in Christ's command to make disciples of all people groups. *Servanthood* is a practical training manual. Its goal is to aid any individual, congregation or organization to get to the next level in Gospel advancement. *Servanthood* will refocus you, from your current level of Gospel engagement to where you should be. You are about to study a planned approach, which covers a wide variety of preparation topics.

Don Jeffreys is a trusted minister of the Gospel with many years of faithful service. *Servanthood* is the result of Don taking on a new challenge as Mission Pastor and not finding specific training materials. What Don has prepared is a well thought out manual with great advice and information. Any individual, church or organization will benefit from this tremendous resource.

Darrell Horn, D. Min.
Executive Director
San Antonio Baptist Association

To Pastors and mission Leaders:

I highly recommend Don Jeffreys and the Servanthood study to you. I met Don in 1990, since that time we have become good friends. He and his church helped me and my church many times through the years.

In 2012, Don joined our staff as pastor of Missions and Senior Adults. When he came on board, we were averaging 2,000 attendees in two worship services, but there was very little going on in the way of missions. Currently, we have approximately 4,000 members, two campuses, four worship services, one in Spanish, and a growing interest following with 300 to 500 viewing our services online each week. Last year we had over 100 candidates for baptism and this year we adopted for the first time a four-million-dollar budget. We believe a significant part of God's blessings and our growth is due to our mission's ministry.

When Don joined our staff, ten per cent of our members were involved in mission work. Now, seven years later, over 40 per cent of our members are involved in some kind of mission work—locally (our Jerusalem), statewide (our Judea), across America (our Samaria) and in seven countries throughout the world. We have over 35 mission ministries where our people are going out and we are still expanding.

Don has compiled and written an outstanding manual called "Servanthood" which he teaches as our mission education once a year. In addition, he leads a Mission's course which we teach once a month to our new members. He faithfully leads a Bible Study called "Lunch with the Lord" every Wednesday at noon. Don supports his pastor, preaches when asked to fill in for me and goes on mission trips representing Resurrection and our Lord.

I urge you to seriously consider receiving Don and the Servanthood study in your church and association.

In His Service,

Ray D. Brown
Senior Pastor
Resurrection Church
Schertz, Texas

My Story

After 50+ years in full-time ministry, I felt the Lord directing me to retire from the pastorate. For years, thinking about this day, I was praying for a place do missions and senior adult work. The day after announcing my resignation, I met up with a dear friend, Pastor Ray Brown. We had known each other, and I had been in the right place at the right time to help him and his church years earlier. We had become good friends, working together in various ministries.

We had not seen each other for a while. He asked about me, and I told him I had just retired. He asked me to make an appointment with his secretary. There he said, "You know, we have a few Anglos in our church." "Yes," I said, "and some other races also." He said, "I want to integrate my church more, but I know I can't do that until I integrate my staff. I believe you have some years left. What would you like to do?"

I thought, "Wow! No one ever asked me what I would like to do in the ministry!" I told him about praying for a place to do missions and senior adult work, but I had no idea where. Most churches raise leaders up from within.

He said, "I don't have a leader for either one. Come on over." So, the next day after I gave in to the Lord, He answered my prayers. Now I am serving on the greatest staff I could have dreamed, being part of Resurrection Church, with two locations, Schertz and San Antonio.

Later, I admitted to my pastor that, as I prayed for a place to serve, the only church that came to mind was Resurrection. But I never thought it was possible, so I never pursued it. Pastor Brown also admitted to me that as he prayed about integrating his staff, he thought about me. But he too, never followed up and the day we met outside Schertz City Hall, he had not planned on inviting me to join his staff. What a joy that we can see the Lord's footprint as we look back!

I came to Resurrection March 27, 2012. The first Sunday I was invited to preach and be introduced. I asked, "How many were involved in a mission experience last year?" With approximately 1200 in attendance in two services, a scattering few raised their hands. We issued the challenge for everyone to go on at least one mission experience. Seven years later, after four of these trainings, we now have more than 1,000 members on at least one mission experience a year. The church has been blessed! We are baptizing over 100 new believers a year; the Kingdom of heaven is expanding locally and beyond. We now have four services each Sunday with a membership of over 5,000 and we believe there are greater things ahead.

What I share in this manual is not from years of experience, but from my first seven years at Resurrection and from the research of others with far more experience. Yet, when I started preparing to train my teams for servanthood, I didn't find a manual or comprehensive instruction anywhere. There is more material available now, but at the time, I didn't find it.

This instruction has received great reviews, some of which you will see in the Foreword and the introductory letter from Pastor Brown, as well as in the following text. It is my prayer that it may be used to help train others who will answer the Lord's call to go and serve, for a day, a week or two, or for the rest of your life. As so many have expressed: The Lord has blessings in store which you will never experience until you go and serve.

Purpose of This Study

Paul Powell, in his book The Last Word, shares a story about a country preacher who went to a convention. Every speaker talked about apathy and lethargy. He wasn't sure what those words meant, but they sounded serious. So, he decided to preach on them. That Sunday, he stood and spoke passionately about both. As he greeted his members after the sermon, one lady asked, "Pastor, you talked about apathy and lethargy. What are they?" He responded, "My dear, don't you know what apathy and lethargy are? Why, they are two of our basic Baptist doctrines."

Powell goes on to say, "Apathy and lethargy are not, of course, Baptist doctrines, but there's an awful lot of both indifference and unconcern in our churches today." My prayer is that this work will challenge and encourage us fellow saints to go out in the fields again to serve – to be found faithful and to make a difference in people's lives.

Isaiah 40:31: But they that wait upon the LORD shall renew their strength; they shall mount up with wings as eagles; they shall run, and not be weary; and they shall walk, and not faint

Pastor Ray Brown likes to say: "The Lord loves you as you are. But He loves you too much to leave you as you are."

How To Study And Teach This Manual

1. Read fully and carefully; highlight specific areas as the Holy Spirit grabs your attention.

2. The manual is organized by sessions (one and a half to two hours each).

3. Leader's Notes are enclosed and highlighted in a box in the Leader's manual which are not found in Student Workbooks.

4. The labs at the end of each session allow practice time for what the class has emphasized.

> I think the training for Missions went very well. It was very informative and organized. This was my first mission trip and I did not know what to expect but...the training and information I received prior to leaving prepared me for the trip.
> —Donna Spillman
> 2014 Mission Trip to Belize

> Sharing info from previous trips helps. Videos/PowerPoints were helpful.
> —Nina Sampson
> 2014 Mission Trip to Haiti

> This class was very informative...it should be kept up – done at least twice a year to get people ready to do God's work.
> —Linda Hawkins
> 2017 Mission Training

Leaders: Have students print their name on the cover with a long blank line for your middle name –
Example: Don _____ Jeffreys. Do you know what goes on the middle line?
Answer - John FLEXIBLE Smith / Jane FLEXIBLE Doe
Flexibility will be discussed later, remember: Servanthood always means being ready for the sudden, unexpected change. Opportunity to serve the Lord often comes at unexpected inconvenient times.

Table of Contents

Leaders note: We recommend starting each session with a devotional and prayer. This may serve as the devotional for this first introductory session

S E S S I O N   1

INTRODUCTION

The Lord's Call

Servanthood centers on the Great Commandment, Great Commission, Great Promise, and Great Assignment

The Great Commandment:

Jesus replied: "'Love the Lord your God with all your heart and with all your soul and with all your mind.' This is the first and greatest commandment. And the second is like it: 'Love your neighbor as yourself.'" Matthew 22:37-39 (NIV)

No mission should ever be undertaken unless and until we have a heart of love – genuine love – for our neighbors, the people God is sending us to.

The Great Commission

Jesus came to them and said, "All authority in heaven and on earth has been given to me. Therefore, go and make disciples of all nations, baptizing them in the name of the Father and of the Son and of the Holy Spirit, and teaching them to obey everything I have commanded you. And surely, I am with you always, to the very end of the age." Matthew 28:18-20 (NIV)

With the Great Commandment and Commission, comes The Great Promise.

The Great Promise: Ye shall receive power, after that the Holy Ghost is come upon you

Jesus said, "But ye shall receive power, after that the Holy Ghost is come upon you: and ye shall be witnesses unto me both in Jerusalem, and in all Judaea, and in Samaria, and unto the uttermost part of the earth" (Acts 1:8 KJV)

First, understand the **promise**; it will give us confidence in obeying the command.

The word means authority. Jews and Greeks understood authority and power were wrapped up in one idea. The power was dunamin (transliteration) power. It is where we get our word dynamite! You will receive dynamite, explosive power! But the promise is conditional upon obeying the command!

Think about the works and miracles of Jesus on earth. He did what He did with heaven's authority. Indeed, the reason He could do the marvels and wonders He did was because He had the authority of God the Father to do it! Now He promises that authority from heaven and that power that is so explosive is available to us – if we carry out the command!

What if I were to tell you that I had placed a million dollars in a certain place for you? It is waiting. You have at your disposal one million dollars. But it is conditional on you going to that place to get it. Though it is yours, it will never be touched or used if you do not go get it. We've got to go to get it! We've got to obey and go where our Lord told us to go if we want the power and authority!

The Great Assignment: ye shall be witnesses unto me both in Jerusalem, and in all Judaea, and in Samaria, and unto the uttermost part of the earth

Finally, understand the Great Command is carried out through the Great Assignment.

Jerusalem – Our town/city

Our Jerusalem is where the Lord has planted us. Find Jerusalem on the map. It is a city. To Jesus' disciples it was where they lived. According to Matthew 28, Jesus sent word to meet Him in Galilee where He gave this command to go back and start where they lived, in Jerusalem! We've got to start at home, where we live, where the Lord has planted us. He planned for us to live where we live, with the family, neighbors and town. He planned for us so to be His representatives – our home and surroundings!

Judea – Our State

Don't stop – go to Judea. The Holy Land map shows Judea is the surrounding state. Our Judea is our state. We must go to our city, but we must also go beyond the city to the state. People in our state are hurting, lonely, disillusioned, despondent, hopeless! God loves them. He is sending us!

Samaria – Our Nation

And then, don't stop – go to Samaria. Again, the map of the Holy Land reveals Samaria is the neighboring state. Galilee, Samaria and Judea, make up the nation of Israel. We can apply this to all of the states within our United States (or whatever country you live in).

World – All Nations

Finally, ye shall be witnesses unto me…unto the uttermost part of the earth. Of course, that's the world. I love to go to the world to preach, teach and witness. But, we cannot, must not, go to the world but not witness where we live! Nor can we be excused by accepting an assignment or two in our city, maybe state, and not caring about people of the world. We must be faithful and obedient to go to all of them!

Take our Lord's Command, Commission, Promise and Assignment SERIOUS and PERSONAL

Personally means – I must believe the Command, Commission, Promise and Assignment are meant for me and our one church. Yes, the Lord's Word is meant for all Christians and all churches, but whether others accept it or not, it is my/our command, commission, our assignment, our promise!

Seriously means – I must get serious about what the Lord has told me/us to do. I cannot excuse myself because some are more gifted, better off financially, educated, or whatever other excuse there may be.

This is my call and assignment. He did not call me/us to go to Jerusalem or Judea or Samaria or… He called and commissioned us to go to Jerusalem **AND** Judea **AND** Samaria **AND**… And I can't excuse myself by saying, "I'll pray for them," or "I'll give an offering." My call and commission are to **GO**.

Evaluation Question: What was the most beneficial (new or best reminders)?
Answer: The translation of the Great Assignment stood out to me.

—Cynthia Gibbs
2017 Mission Training

Disciples

Our desire is to go and make disciples. At the same time, become better, growing disciples ourselves.

Make Disciples

There are many great agencies that do great work for mankind. And we want to be part of that. The Bible teaches us to care for the whole man – body, mind and spirit. We care about their physical needs, just as Jesus did! But that's not our ultimate aim. As one put it, "You came and helped me get out of poverty, but I'm still going to hell."

Always remember that Jesus commanded us to go and **MAKE DISCIPLES**, not just to do good humanitarian deeds, not even just to make converts. We want to build relationships, not just "win 'em and drop 'em." Relationships will last and we hope contacts that will continue long after we are gone from their physical presence. But remember as someone has so accurately said, "We haven't made a disciple until the person you led to the Lord is making disciples."

Become Better, Growing Disciples

While working to make disciples of others, we ourselves are always in a constant state of **GROWING** in the Lord. Our desire is to put more missionaries on the field. But we recognize that not everyone is ready for an overseas mission trip. Some need to start at home. Others are ready to grow and go on a trip to work and minister outside of home, yet not yet on the foreign field.

We challenge our people to go on a mission trip in **EACH** of the four areas of our Lord's commission. Our assignment is not Jerusalem or Judea or Samaria or the world, but Jerusalem and Judea and Samaria and the world. Yet not everyone is on the same plane in their missional vision, confidence or maturity. We are not all ready to go off, but we can all serve – somewhere, in some way, to make a difference in someone's life for the Lord.

Missions Ministry God's Hands

Invariably, when we ask what church members understand of missions, they reply with something like "going overseas" or "giving to our foreign missions offering." Very few really get the concept that Servanthood to the people we live and work around and throughout our state, nation, and world is all part of our responsibility as servants of our Lord Jesus. All of this is part of our commission.

The diagram on the right show the ministries we call Servanthood or Missions and with these ministries we try to attack our assignment in the four areas of the Great Commission

LAB WORK

Scriptural Basis for Missions: In small groups of three or four, discuss the following Scriptures. Look at the texts from two sets of eyes:

1. How does this Scripture apply to me personally?
2. How do I see this Scripture applying to my involvement in an upcoming mission trip?

Share with each other. Select a group leader and share the highlights of your discussion with the class.

Acts 1:8   Mark 10:43-45   Isaiah 6:8

> Leader: 1) Do not feel that you have to use all the Scriptures
>   2) Feel free to select other appropriate Scriptures
>   3) Use as many of these lab assignments as time allows for your setting

Review Your Church's Trip Agreement – See Appendix 3: Read Trip Agreement in unison

Think Through Dr. King's Statement – Place different opportunities for service in each category:

— What service opportunities would you consider crawling experiences (So easy everyone can do it)?
— What service opportunities would you consider walking experiences (A step above crawl stage)?
— What service opportunities would you consider running (A little more discipline, struggle)?
— What service opportunities would you consider flying? (Hardest, most disciplined to get into)?

HOMEWORK

Review the Introduction – what were some of the highlights you want to remember?

Review and Learn our Church Vision, Purpose and Mission Statements (p. 8)

Read Chapter 1 (Pencil in answers you anticipate)

Bring to Class Next Session:
Bible and Pen
Personal Calendar
I-phone or Android with downloaded 1Cross app
Humble Spirit

> Leader: Ask one of your participants for each session to prepare a devotional for the next session and each session thereafter. This helps with participation. They may want to read Scripture, pray, give a 10 minute devotional and/or lead the group in a chorus.

Evaluation Question: Overall what did we do well? I thought the information sharing was very good. Having people participate in Labs was very important.

—Chris Evans
2017 Mission Training

Leader: Brainstorm briefly: What was the #1 take-away from the Introduction – Session 1?

SESSION 2

Devotional and Prayer

GETTING READY BY UNDERSTANDING

Understand our Mission

1. Remember our overall VISION

Never stray from your church vision/mission statement – who and what we are!

2. Be a TEAM

T = TEAMWORK: We are a team! Pitch in, help, don't wait for others. Go the extra mile.
E = ENCOURAGEMENT: Encourage teammates. Keep your words positive. Build others up.
A = ATTITUDE: Watch your attitude – especially in tough times.
M = MISSION: Mission is #1. Your needs and desires must take a back seat to the mission.

Commit to this ideal: For the duration of this trip I will submit to my mission, team and leaders

Make every missionary feel like they are part of the mission. BE A TEAM.

—Sheron Green
2014 Mission Trip to Belize

3. RBC's Mission Picture, Purpose and Goals

The Goal: For every member involved in at least one mission/outreach activity every year.

The Idea: Provide mission trips to each of the four areas of our Lord's Acts 1:8 commission.

The Need: The need is worldwide, and the opportunities are endless.

The Partnership: Coordinate with an organization or leader on the ground 3 or more months out.

The Plan: Make preliminary investigative trips as necessary.

The Vision: Continue to enlarge mission ministries everywhere possible.

The Cost: Members pay their own expenses supported by a budget and scholarships.

The Benefits: 1. Untold lives touched by example and witness!
2. Members coming back more consecrated and committed!
3. Joy in fulfilling our Lord's commission/assignment!

4. Plan for an End Result – EXIT STRATEGY

Saddleback Church has an excellent plan for an exit strategy called the PEACE Plan. We'll give you a gist here. We recommend of Saddleback Church, to get more in depth training.

Step 1: Start the foundation: go, see the need, build relationships
Step 2: Teach local believers
Step 3: Equip local people who are capable of being local leaders and trainers
Step 4: Give resources to leaders as necessary – literature, building materials, etc.
Step 5: Step away and turn work over to the locals. This is planned in advance but reevaluated as necessary. Of course, some ministries are forever ongoing.

Of course, be aware that some ministries are forever ongoing.

**The exit strategy for some is the coming of the Lord in the clouds of glory –
or an exit strategy for that particular trip rather than an exit strategy for
ending the mission work in that place and not coming back**

5. Know your purpose – MISSION OBJECTIVE

Each Mission Trip Team will declare its own mission objective statement

Your specific mission trip should have a stated objective that everyone understands –

Why are you going?
What do you hope and plan to accomplish?

_____

_____

_____

_____

Evaluation Question: How effective do you feel your team was in accomplishing your mission?
Answer: Very effective, the Word was shared and projects completed. Evening debriefs were necessary and helpful.
—Don Young
2014 Mission Trip to Haiti

Mission trips are very important. I really feel that we need to realize this is not a vacation, but a working mission trip. That it is not about us. We are the body of Christ, and we all have a part to do. We must decrease so that Jesus can increase. That should be expressed in our training.
—Sheron Green
2014 Mission Trip to Belize

Understand our Witness

Why do we Go?

1. **We go to <u>SHARE CHRIST</u>!** Look for opportunities to witness – everywhere, every day!

We do not go just to do good humanitarian work, but to share the gospel! If we are told that we cannot witness your leaders will choose one of two strategies:

#1: Tell the organization leaders upfront that sharing Christ is our #1 objective. If they do not want us to do so, it's OK; there are other organizations, churches and mission works.

Or #2: Go ahead and serve with the organization, but look for witnessing opportunities outside of the organizations boundary – outside their buildings, at the hotel, as you shop or go to meals, etc.

2. **We go to <u>SUPPORT AND ENCOURAGE OUR HOST MISSIONARIES</u>!**
   We must leave such a good reputation and report that:

   a. We are invited back.
   b. Our host will have open doors to minister when we leave.

Do not underestimate this critical part of our mission purpose.

3. **We go to <u>LEARN</u>**

One of the misguided understandings of people going on service trips is that we are going to show the poor how to do things. We need to incorporate them in the work with us – not do it for them! And we need to learn from them! One of the best techniques for learning is — ask questions and listen!

4. **We do not go to <u>VACATION or HOLIDAY</u>!**

Lake Providence LA., 2012

We debrief – but it's not vacation. We try to arrange for the final day to be relaxing and debrief. We may find a place to shop, beach, tour or just to lie around and play games. At noon or in the evening, we plan a good lunch or dinner and debrief. Debriefing is an important reflective time.

> Leaders: In debriefing, stay positive. Be sensitive to areas of weakness to improve on for future trips. Remember: you want your team to come back positive and encourage others at home.

Debriefing on the mission field may not always be possible. We try our best to get the team together before going home.

Who Can Go?

A. Your team leader should have <u>CLEAR STANDARDS</u> for answering this question.

B. <u>SERVANTS</u> can go!

Feed My Starving Children, 2017

C. **An Atheist Who Went on a Mission Trip** — <u>Oct 28</u> by <u>awakensa</u> (2011)

I'm sure you re-read the title. "An atheist on a mission trip?"

"There must be some catch. You're talking about a professing Christian who was living life as a practical atheist and went on a mission trip and rediscovered the importance of truly living by faith, right?" No, although that happens all the time.

An actual atheist went on a mission trip with BSM a few weeks ago. Specifically to Bastrop to help with clean up from the fire ravaged community. Surprising isn't it?

I am so proud of our students and leaders. They take the Great Commission seriously. They are intentionally leaving the Christian sub-culture of 'safety' and going to where the lost are, and engaging them in relationships. Through intentional, loving relationships our students and staff and leaders are engaging the lost and the lost are responding. My first post was about BSM's commitment to the Great Commission, to make disciples, to leave the 99 to pursue the 1, and this is just an example (among many) of what our students are doing.

The atheist did not come to Christ. Has not…yet. Oh, did I mention this atheist is also the president of his atheist organization? And did I mention that he actually came to a BSM worship service? Oh, and did I mention that he comes to lunch and hears Scripture and Gospel weekly?

The Atheist Who Went on a Mission Trip is a work in progress. I do not feel comfortable sharing his name. God knows him and now you know he exists as well. You know he is a "soul in process." Pray for his salvation. Pray for our students. What they are doing is truly remarkable.

Churches-we could all learn a lot from what our students are doing on our campuses. Intentionality, Relationships, Commitment to the Great Commission.

Where do we Go?

THE NEEDIEST OF THE NEEDY!

James 2:5: Listen, my dear brothers and sisters: Has not God chosen those who are poor in the eyes of the world to be rich in faith and to inherit the kingdom he promised those who love him?

James 2:6: But you have dishonored the poor. Is it not the rich who are exploiting you? Are they not the ones who are dragging you into court?

People live in the most humble and unsanitary conditions imaginable, and the gospel admonishes us to remember to care for the poor, needy and oppressed (Gal. 2:9-10).

But the fact is the **LOST** are the neediest of the needy! The lost may be rich or poor, here or there, great or peasant, etc. The lost need to be reached whoever and wherever they are.

> LEADER: If you have specific mission trip plans, this would be a good place to share them.
> **a.** Share where they are going
> **b.** Share why that place has been chosen
> **c.** What team meetings will be expected after theses general sessions.

What do we go to Proclaim?

Know **THE GOSPEL** so you can share it!

A – **ADMIT** your **SIN**!

B – **BELIEVE** in the **LORD JESUS CHRIST**!

C – **CONFESS** that Jesus is now your **LORD**

When does our Witness Matter?

Carrefour, Haiti, 2012

   1. **Among our own team members – PEOPLE WE WORK AROUND!**

John 13:35: By this everyone will know that you are my disciples, if you **love** one another."

Romans 12:10 Be **devoted** to one another in **love**. **Honor** one another above yourselves.

1 Thessalonians 4:9 Now about your **love** for one another we do not need to write to you, for you yourselves have been taught by God to **love** each other.

2. Host nation – <u>PEOPLE WE WORK AMONG!</u>

Hebrews 13:17: Have confidence in your leaders and **submit** to their authority, because they keep watch over you as those who must give an account. Do this so that their work will be a joy, not a burden, for that would be of no benefit to you

3. Host nation – <u>PEOPLE WE WORK WITH!</u>

1 Peter 2:13-14: **Submit** yourselves for the Lord's sake to every human authority: whether to the emperor, as the supreme authority, [14] or to governors, who are sent by him to punish those who do wrong and to commend those who do right.

4. **Our Witness Plans** – Be familiar with several which you may choose from – we offer three here:

A. <u>1CROSS.COM</u> – Personal testimonies in many languages. Download App and practice using it.

Vista Community Church, Temple, TX, in Honduras, 2011

B. <u>TRACTS</u> – Prepared in the language where you serve. Practice using tracts everywhere.

Why use tracts?

Surveys show: for every 5,000 tracts given someone places faith in Jesus. Scatter seed, broadcast!

How do I use tracts?

➢ Thank You tracts to anyone who does a service – with a generous tip.
➢ Witness tracts everywhere. Ask if you can share a good word. When possible take time to read it.
➢ Give tracts at hospital and convalescent home visits. If folks are asleep, I never wake them (though some have sort of scolded me when I come back because I didn't). I feel that if they are asleep, they probably need it and the last thing I want is to interrupt their recovery sleep. But I will leave a tract with a note on the bottom or on the back saying that I'm sorry I missed them but hoping the words in the tract will be helpful and meaningful. When I go back to see them, I will ask if they read it and what they think, and if possible read it over again with them.
➢ Whenever we go overseas, we try to get one of our witness tracts printed in a parallel version with English and the language of the nation we are going to. We take 500 or more with us and encourage our team to use them throughout our stay in the nation we visit.

Tracts are potentially one of the most powerful witnesses we can give. We give the tract and trust the Lord to do His work through the Holy Spirit! You can get Christian witness tracts online, or at any Christian book store and they are reasonably cheap to purchase.

C. BRIDGE ILLUSTRATION

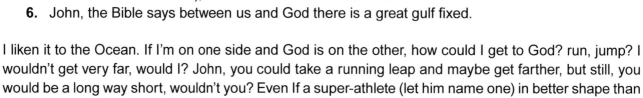

1. Draw two blocks and enter God and man over the blocks
2. Change "Man" to person's name you are speaking with (ex: John)
3. Ask John for his understanding of God – simple, one-word descriptions.
4. Use John's words for God and enter them under "God" on the right.
5. Ask John this: "Compared to God, what is man? God is Holy (or whatever word he used), what is man? Go down the list
6. John, the Bible says between us and God there is a great gulf fixed.

I liken it to the Ocean. If I'm on one side and God is on the other, how could I get to God? run, jump? I wouldn't get very far, would I? John, you could take a running leap and maybe get farther, but still, you would be a long way short, wouldn't you? Even If a super-athlete (let him name one) in better shape than both of us tried, could he/she make it to God's side? Of course not.

So, John, how can we get to God's side? There is only one way. And Jesus paid the price to make it possible. (Complete drawing the cross)

7. Ask two questions:

1) John, do you believe Jesus died for your sins on the cross and rose on the third day?
2) John, would you like to be saved right now?

The tools for sharing the Gospel were very good!

—Chris Evans
2017 Mission Training

Evaluation Question: What was the most beneficial (new or best reminders)?
Answer: I loved the example of the "Bridge" an easy personal tract.

—Lolly Faison
2017 Mission Training

Understand our Expectations

Expect a <u>BACKGROUND CHECK</u> *Which most organizations now require*

Know the <u>FINANCIAL COST</u> *Which you are usually expected to raise*

Take along some extra <u>MONEY</u> *Which you will spend on souvenirs, possibly travel, etc.*

Be Prepared for <u>RUSTIC CONDITIONS</u> *Which will likely have no TV, nor possibly hot water.*

Hotels will not be Five-Star accommodations. Be prepared to take short, cold showers. Often water is at a premium. Often air conditioning is not offered, or electricity may go on and off. Have a flashlight and a battery-operated fan

Family home on Belo Mountain, Haiti

Even after all this training, we still have received evaluations that commented about how standards were just not "acceptable."

> Lodging at the (Motel named) was not only a waste of resources, it was also far below lodging standards we should have been forced to accept…The room I stayed in did not have hot water during my stay; therefore, I had to go to another room to take a hot shower. Our beds were NOT made up or towels exchanged out every day. Several days upon returning from our missionary duties, we had to request clean sheets and for the beds to be made up and clean towels!! The ice machine was not working most of the time we were there. The Wi-Fi connectivity did not work properly from our room and a new password had to be requested daily from the Front Desk. If we were to stay in an upgraded facility, better logistical research should have been done to ensure the accommodations were satisfying…We should receive a refund…During these five days, we were forced to eat Oriental food three days!!...the food was not tasty at all. As seasoned travelers, we should have been afforded an opportunity to select what kind of food wanted to eat during our stay
>
> --Anonymous

It should also be noted that others have come back somewhat disappointed because they went expecting to sacrifice in rough conditions and found hotels and conveniences far better than they expected.

Get Your <u>MEDICAL RELEASE</u> *Which you might not need, but is always a good idea*

Let your doctor know where you are going. Get him/her to sign the Doctor's Medical release. Also fill out your own medical record and release.

Obviously, for most day trips medical releases will not be necessary, but always a good idea. You never know what might happen.

Get into the Culture:

Again, we remind you to **PREPARE YOURSELF** for the experience. Do not rely on this training.

It is imperative for **EVERYONE** be familiar with the cultural values of those you will be working among. A great project can be damaged irreparably by offending people with whom you will be working.

Go to the INTERNET or YOUTUBE and look up the place you will serve, the specific area if possible.

Language hindrances, Logistics, Health Care, etc. along with Mission or Service Agreements should be discussed in team meetings prior to leaving

Spend Time with the **PEOPLE** Which is the reason for your servanthood

Resurrection Ministries with Haitians on Belo Mountain, Haiti, 2014

1. Remember we are going to minister to and serve **THEM**. Every day look for someone put in your path for His divine purpose. Witness to him or her.

2. Think about your **MISSIONARIES** What you can do to encourage and build them up?

3. Be **UNDERSTANDING**. We team up with other organizations and ministries besides with the people we go to serve

4. Be **PATIENT**. We don't always agree with the way others do things. Patience is a real virtue. Everybody respects a person who shows much patience.

Be FLEXIBLE

There is a reason for placing you in team on which you are asked to serve. Likewise, if asked to shift to another team, for a day or two, or for the duration of the trip, there is a reason. Please be available, to your leaders. Remember we are going to help the people and our host/s on the field – which means:

1. Your assignment may change
2. Your schedule may change
3. Your transportation may change – possibly even walk instead of ride
4. Your accommodations may change

Be Faithful to all
TEAM AND TRAINING MEETINGS

These training sessions will not be the only meetings you will be expected to attend. As you focus in on your particular trip, specific training and team meetings relating to that trip will be required

Team meeting before trip, Belize, 2014

LAB WORK

Scriptural Basis for Missions: In small groups of three or four, discuss the following Scriptures. Look at the texts from two sets of eyes:

1. How does this Scripture apply to me personally?
2. How do I see this Scripture applying to my involvement in an upcoming mission trip?

Share with each other. Select a group leader and share the highlights of your discussion with the class.

John 6:5-13   Matthew 5:14-16   John 15:8-17

Leader:	1) Do not feel that you have to use all the Scriptures 2) Feel free to select other appropriate Scriptures 3) Use as many of these lab assignments as time allows for your setting

Review Your Church's Trip Agreement – Appendix 3: Divide the class and read Trip Agreement in parts

Practice Being A Witness: — Download and practice using 1Cross.com
Practice w/Tracts
Practice w/Bridge Illustration

Practice Encouraging our Hosts: Break up in pairs and find something about the other person to encourage him/her about!

HOMEWORK

Review chapter 2 – what were some of the highlights you want to remember?

Review and Learn our Church Vision, Purpose and Mission Statements (p. 8)

Read chapter 3 – (Pencil in answers you anticipate)

Bring to Class Next Session: Bible and Pen
Personal Calendar
I-phone or Android with downloaded 1Cross app
Humble Spirit

Evaluation Question: What can we do to improve – answer: Practice, Practice, Practice and stay in prayer.

—Oletia Bethea
2014 Mission Trip to Haiti

Evaluation Question: What was the most beneficial (new or best reminders) you received?
Answer: I enjoyed the moment when we were asked to share the Gospel with partners

—Gregorio A. Armand
2017 Mission Training

Leader: Brainstorm briefly: What was the #1 take-away from Session 2?

SESSION 3

Devotional and Prayer

GETTING READY PERSONALLY

Personal **CALENDAR** – Dates, Plan of approach

Examples of dates to include: Insert…

Training dates Due dates of financial obligations Prayer partner meeting dates Team meeting dates	Prayer and fasting dates Dates to have supplies ready and packed Date to start spraying clothes	Dates to make announcements to other ministries or organizations Date of commissioning by the church

Place your calendar in a prominent place where you will necessarily look at it every day to be reminded:

1. Do Not to allow other appointments to interfere with preparation and training dates
2. Be reminded to attend training and team meetings
3. Be reminded to pray about your servanthood trip

Leader: Discussion of Passport/Visa is not in Student Manual. It might be good to give a brief synopsis here and urge everyone to get a Passport now and have it ready.

Personal **PASSPORT/VISA** – Acquiring Passport/Visa, Three Copies

What is the difference between a passport and a visa? Passports are for **SHORT-TERM** trips outside the United States. Visas are for **EXTENDED** stays, usually more than thirty days

To get a passport, go to your nearest Post Office. They will direct you. Passports take time to get. Plan at least six months out (earlier is even better). It probably will not take that long to receive your passport, but things happen, strikes, government shut-downs, lost paperwork…

A Visa must be obtained from the country you plan to enter. Not all countries require a Visa. Be sure you know if you must have one. Check with the United States embassy in the nation where you plan to travel. Again, Visas are generally required for extended stays of more than thirty days.

YOUR PASSPORT NEEDS TO BE VALID FOR AT LEAST <u>6-MONTHS</u> AFTER YOUR PLANNED RETURN HOME.

On our application to go on a mission or servanthood trip, we require that our applicants put down the date their passport expires. This way they must look at their passport and know it will be good for the dates we will be overseas.

Before we thought to make this part of our application process, one year we had a man who made all the preparations, then two weeks before we were to travel called me to let me know that his passport was due to expire while we would have been in the foreign country.

We recommend making <u>THREE (3)</u> copies of your passport –

1. One is turned in with your application to be kept in file at home.
2. One is to hide away in your carry-on case.
3. One is to store away in your luggage.

If your passport is damaged, water logged, lost or stolen, you will not be able to get back on the airplane to get home until it is replaced. You will need to go to an American Embassy in the country where you are and apply for a replacement, and having a copy of your old one will expedite the process.

As we said, a Visa is generally required when you plan to work or stay in a country for an extended time. This is also one reason we never say we are entering a country for work or on a mission. When you fill out forms to enter a country put down that you are there for personal reasons or as a tourist.

Personal Comfort

Our <u>TRAVEL</u>

Tap Tap community transportation, Haiti

1. We may travel in rough vehicles or over rough terrain. Be prepared!

2. Walking may be necessary – a lot of walking!

3. Spend time <u>EXERCISING</u>, walking and getting in physical shape before leaving.

Our HEALTH

Leader: Some of this material may be repeated, but it is so crucial that those going on short-term service assignments understand the great importance!

Get a health CHECK-UP

See your doctor. Get release and recommendations for shots and meds. Ask for a prescription of Cipro and Imodium or other drugs you will need if you start symptoms of nausea, diarrhea, or general weakness.

Start EXERCISING. This may not sound like important preparation, but most people find servanthood trips more physically taxing than they thought. We walk or stand on your feet. We have even climbed mountains.

Keep WELL

Five Guidelines about FOOD AND WATER – Follow strictly the guidelines of your leader.

Hogs in village, Honduras

1. Do not **DRINK** the water or any liquid, unless you check with team leader and/or our host.

2. Our **HOSTS WILL PROVIDE** safe drinking water.

3. Do not **RINSE YOUR TOOTHBRUSH** in water or hydrant.

4. Do not eat **UNCOOKED/UNPEELED** fruits or vegetables

5. Do not eat **ANYTHING OFFERED BY NATIVE PEOPLE** unless it is approved by your team leader our host.

When gracious native people offer you something to eat, accept it graciously, but do not eat it. Tell them you are committed to a team meal, but you would like to take it with you. You can discard it later or give it to another native of the area (and be careful even about this). .

When possible, we like to take one of our own medical professionals on our trips with us for minor medical needs among our team members.

Know the CUSTOMS/CULTURE

In many places folks **get only ONE or TWO meals per day**, and often not for sumptuous consumption, but sustenance. Take **SNACKS** for between meals.

Special precautions:

1. **Never eat in the <u>PRESENCE</u> of natives who do not get an extra meal each day.**

2. Similarly, when <u>CLEAN WATER</u> is a premium, **never ask a native to get you a drink.** Remember that they are limited in the amount of water they may get to drink each day.

3. **Avoid <u>ICE</u>, <u>SALADS</u>, any fresh <u>VEGETABLES</u> (uncooked), <u>RE-HEATED</u> foods, uncooked <u>SHELLFISH</u>, fruit not <u>PEELED</u>, food from <u>STREET VENDORS</u>.**

01/02/2010 PM 11:37

Honduras, 2011

4. **Reminder to drink only water <u>BOTTLED</u> or <u>BOILED</u> or <u>PROVIDED</u> by our hosts**

5. **Soft drinks are generally OK also, unless warned against them by your host.**

But What If You Become <u>ILL</u> or <u>INJURED</u>

1. **Your team leader should be able to explain what procedures are in place.**

2. We ask that **each team leader provide for a basic first aid kit** to take with your team.

3. <u>**Our Policy**</u> – On any given day, if you wake up feeling <u>WEAK</u> or a little <u>NAUSEATED</u>, or with even a little diarrhea — <u>NOTIFY</u> **your team leader**. Do not be embarrassed or let your manly willpower tempt you not to tell!

We are guided by the following procedure:

a. We will not take you out on assignment that day.

It is important that you **DO NOT ALLOW** yourself to let your system get more run down, and that you **DO NOT EXPOSE** any of your team nor natives of the land to what you may have started coming down with. We would rather you stay back one day, rest and refresh.

b. But we will not leave you alone.

Someone on the team, chosen by **YOUR TEAM LEADER** will be asked to stay with you.

This is another reason to be sure you bring plenty of <u>LEISURE READING MATERIAL</u>

Evaluation Question: What was the most beneficial (new or best reminders)?
Answer: Very informative about things we need to do to get ready for mission work: have passport, plan, take care of your health.

—Clisher Harmon
2017 Mission Training

Our SERVICE AGREEMENTS

Most of the time we are given an agreement to sign or instructions to follow provided by our host missionaries or organization where we serve. It is an important document. If one exists be aware of it and be familiar with the terms. It was signed by your leader or our administration for your team. Your trip leader will make it part of your training for your specific trip.

In addition, we have our own Trip Agreement Form. We go over it in our LABS after one or more of the sessions. You must sign the form signifying your agreement to the terms. (Appendix 2)

Our ATTIRE

We always want to represent our LORD and our CHURCH through our clothing! Many of our work sites and partnership agreements also have dress codes which we must be aware of and affirm. Please be aware –

No ALCOHOL ads

No SEXUALLY SUGGESTIVE attention getters

No POLITICAL attire!

No MILITARY attire!

A couple of examples of dress requirements from some of our partner organizations:

Haven for Hope – No spaghetti strap shirts, tanks, shorts/skirts shorter than knee high, skirts shorter than waist length or pants below the waist.

Habitat for Humanity – Comfortable clothes appropriate for the work and weather. Wear items that can get stained, ripped, muddy, paint-spackled, etc. You must wear closed-toed shoes – do not wear flip flops, backless shoes or Crocs. For safety, do not wear loose, oversized clothing or dangling jewelry. Summer months can be extremely hot, and it can get very cold on site in the winter. Dress appropriately.

Church Clothes: long pants, polo or collared shirts for men and dress or skirt for women; Please do not wear shorts or t-shirts to the church service and shoulders should be covered. Some men may like to wear a tie.

Leisure Clothes: shorts, pants, decent shirts, sandals. Please wear tank tops only in the hotel and beach. Most people wear shorts to bed. If you need to use the bathroom at night, then you could be in public walking to them.

Personal Sacrifice

LEADERS: While this particularly deals with overnight trips, some of these ideas could certainly apply to shorter, even local trips and may be worth spending time to talk about in class

Leave at Home:

Do Not Bring <u>LARGE BILLS</u> – ($20's, 50's, and 100's).

Do Not Bring Expensive <u>JEWELRY</u>

Buy a cheap watch and imitation jewelry, or better, no jewelry. Even cheap jewelry, do not bring flashy or attention-getting jewelry. There is a fair chance it could be stolen, or you could be targeted.

Leave your <u>HAIR DRYER</u> at home!

Leave a complete <u>ITINERARY</u> with a friend or family member back home

Turn in the name and email address of <u>ONE (1)</u> contact person to your team leader In case of emergencies, the team leader will make one call to someone back home.

Do Not Bring Anything you would <u>HATE TO LOSE</u>

Remove anything in your wallet or purse that will not be needed on the trip.

Do not bring or wear <u>FATIGUES</u> or <u>MILITARY</u> clothing

This has already been discussed, but it bears repeating!

Avoid Wearing <u>PERFUME</u>

You will stand out and draw mosquitos. On one mission trip, I followed behind a lady in our group who was wearing very sweet-smelling and noticeable perfume. I watched as the native men she passed stopped, turned and watched her pass by and often whispered among themselves.

We recommend that you do not bring <u>ELECTRONIC</u> equipment

(Computers, iPod, expensive cameras, etc.) – If you do (warning!) These items, if left around, will "walk". Keep in mind that <u>you bring them at your own risk</u>. If you bring them, do not forget to bring extra batteries and keep them with you or hidden away at all times.

Also, please limit your time on the internet to brief emails and Facebook post/blog updates. Part of the experience of a mission trip is to unplug from the world as we know it – "when in Rome…"

By all means, leave the <u>SELFIE STICK</u> at home!

It's not about you; it's about the Lord and His work! Do not give the impression to those you work with or around that you want pictures of yourself to show the good folks back home how you went to work among these the poor, needy natives in _____ country.

LAB WORK

Scriptural Basis for Missions: In small groups of three or four, discuss the following Scriptures. Look at the texts from two sets of eyes:

1) How does this Scripture apply to me personally?
2) How do I see this Scripture applying to my involvement in an upcoming mission trip?

Share with each other. Select a group leader and share the highlights of your discussion with the class.

Proverbs 22:9   Matthew 25:31-40   Matthew 22:37-40

> Leader: 1) Do not feel that you have to use all the Scriptures
>   2) Feel free to select other appropriate Scriptures
>   3) Use as many of these lab assignments as time allows for your setting

Review Resurrection's Trip Agreement – See Appendix 3

Men read together odd numbers (1, 3, 5, 7, 9)
Ladies read together even numbers (2, 4, 6, 8, 10)

Practice Being A Witness
— Download and practice using 1Cross.com
— Practice w/Tracts
— Practice w/Bridge Illustration

Practice Encouraging our Hosts

Break up in pairs and find something the other person has to encourage him/her about!

Evaluation Question: What did we do well?
Answer: Sharing past experiences. Lab work

—Terry Hughes
2017 Mission Training

HOMEWORK

Review chapter 3 – what were some of the highlights you want to remember?

Review and Learn our Church Vision, Purpose and Mission Statements (p. 8)

Read chapter 4
(Pencil in answers you anticipate)

Bring to Class Next Session: Bible and Pen
Personal Calendar
I-phone or Android with downloaded 1Cross app
Humble Spirit

Leader: Brainstorm briefly: What was the #1 take-away from Session 3?

SESSION 4

Devotional and Prayer

GETTING READY SPIRITUALLY

Evaluation Question: What was the most beneficial (new or best reminders)?
Answer: Devotional and prayers.

—Rhonda Harris
2016 Mission Training

Spiritual Accountability

Keep up with your DEVOTIONAL TIME

Your **devotional time** is primary for life as a Christian as well as for mission work.

Paul Powell, The Last Word says (p. 28), "if we want to return to our first love, we need to wait quietly. We must not get so busy working for Him that we have no time to spend with Him...that means we must have a time of private prayer and Bible study, and we can't just breeze in and blow off steam. We've got to spend some quiet time with Him."

Nothing is more important than your GROWING RELATIONSHIP with the Lord. When you return from your service, you should be closer to the Lord than ever – and keep growing. If you do not have a personal devotional time every day with the Lord now, please start now!

Journal:

1. Even if you don't keep a personal diary, there will be EXPERIENCES you will want to remember. There will likely be many experiences that it will be easy to forget when, where, names, etc. – even some.

2. Be ready to GIVE AN ACCOUNT to family, prayer partners and others. Journaling helps

3. Also be prepared because you may be asked to give TESTIMONIES to other groups

Church members are interested in your work. You are likely to get invitations to share experiences with the church body, and various ministries in the church.

Members also get invitations to share with civic organizations and charities – another awesome opportunity to share witness with your community!

Evaluation Question: What was the most beneficial (new or best reminders)?
Answer: Encouraged me to step up devotions.

—Belinda Evans
2018 Mission Training

Spiritual Praying

PRAYER PARTNERS are critical to our success

Prayer is a vital KEY of all of our mission trips.

Prayer partners are part of our TEAM even though they don't make the trip with us.

You may have as many prayer partners as you wish, but we ask that you turn in the names of two (only two). Why two? We contact prayer partners to urge upon them the seriousness of their investment and ask them to do some special things. Too many names make it hard to contact and work with everyone.

Before you fill out the prayer partner page, don't assume – ask the person if he/she is willing to serve as a prayer partner for you. Let them know that you need serious prayer partners. There are several things we will ask of prayer partners. Tell them they will be contacted. Tell them that you want to pray with them on a regular basis (at least once a week) before you leave. Also let them know that they are welcome to come to any of your team meetings (including our training sessions) to know better how to pray for you and what is being expected of you. Also let them know that you particularly want them to come to your team's time of fasting and prayer. Give them the date, time and place of that prayer retreat.

After you ask if they are seriously willing and they agree, turn in the names of two Prayer Partners

Then, remember your prayer partners as you are on the trip. They are praying for you; you pray for them. If you have a chance to buy personal souvenirs, remember their faithfulness back home.

Leaders: Information To Share With Prayer Partners

If you lead multiple teams or large groups, you may want to assign a Prayer Partner Team Leader.

When you contact Prayer Partners, here are a few things you might want to share:

1. Emphasize that they are part of our team even though they are not making the trip with us.

2. We want them to pray with their missionary/servants on a regular basis (at least once a week) before you leave and certainly continue, preferably daily, all through the time we are gone. Give them a devotional guide so they can do the same devotionals you will be doing.

3. We invite them to come to any of your team meetings to know better how to pray for their missionary/servants and what is being expected.

4. We particularly want them to come to your team's time of fasting and prayer

5. I always like to ask prayer partners to write a letter to their missionary, but not tell them. They should give it to you or your assigned person responsible for this ministry.

Then distribute the letter about mid-week during the team's trip, or after a day that has possibly been especially hard, frustrating or dangerous.

Those who have gone with me before begin to know this is coming and look forward to it. For those who are going for the first time, or may have forgotten that I distribute mail, this is a pleasant surprise.

Pray together AS A TEAM and pray FOR YOUR TEAM

DAILY in Your Prayer and Devotional Time

Not only should you spend time praying with your team, but also for your team. This should be a regular and daily appointment you have with the Lord up until and through the time you leave.

REGULARLY in Your Team Meetings

Before we stated that you must not only pray with your team, but for your team. Now we reverse that – not only should you spend time praying for your team, but also with your team. Certainly, this should be done in each session, when your team comes together for preparation. But it should also be done in your own personal prayer and devotional time.

Disaster Relief, Moore, OK., 2013

Get serious about praying about your Lord's assignment and those assigned to go out with you!

OFTEN in special times of Prayer and Fasting

Some service ministries recommend fasting and prayer

Belize Team Mtg., 2014

at regular, weekly times. Most of the time they do not come together, but encourage each participant to commit to pray and fast at a certain time or day of each week up until the team leaves on the trip.

We recommend a prayer and fasting retreat before you leave. Bring the prayer partners together with the team (we even invite others from the church to come). We have had some of our best comments from trip evaluations to be about the time they spent in prayer and fasting.

> I will never forget what Bro. Don taught us about how to study the Bible during our prayer and fasting. It will stay with me forever.
>
> —Priscilla Armstrong
> 2014 Mission Trip to Haiti

CONTINUE while on the Field

Teams are encouraged to pray and prepare together EACH EVENING while you are on the field. Each team leader is asked to prepare or assign a short devotional for each evening after work is completed for the day. Then spend a few moments debriefing your team. What were the highs and lows? What did each team member learn or gain? How did he or she grow spiritually in the Lord? Did you see God using hard situations for the good and glory of the Kingdom?

We recommend your team pray **at least once** EACH DAY before you board the vehicles for your daily trip to the worksite, or after debriefing each evening.

Ideas for Remembering Your Prayer Partners:

1. BEFORE you go

Set regular prayer times with prayer partners. Do not let them become social times, nor times to skip. Plan a prayer and fasting retreat with your team together.

> Evaluation Question: What did we do well? Answer: …having prayer partners to come fast with us
>
> —Steve Bethea
> 2014 Mission Trip to Haiti

2. AS you go

Remember to pray for them when you are anxious, facing trial or temptation, They are praying for you. Call or drop them a card soon after arriving so they will receive it half-way into your time. A souvenir card reminds them also.

3. When you RETURN

Remember to bring them back some trinket or souvenir, a "thank you" for their prayers, and a report of work and needs where served. People's needs are ongoing.

01/02/2010 AM 06:20

Medical Team praying with client, Honduras, 2011

Ask OTHERS to pray

Ask family, friends, and others to pray for you! Of your two prayer partners, one may be family. Others do not have to attend all the meetings, but would pray, especially financial donors.

Spiritual Assessment

Team Debrief Haiti, 2012

At the end of the trip – DEBRIEF

I like to take **the last day of a trip to relax, debrief as a group**, and share together before we start our trip back home. Sometimes this will not be possible. You may need to meet as a team again after you get back home for this purpose, or to assess and start the planning and preparing for the next trip. Again, if you know this is likely, plan and calendar the meeting before you leave.

Spiritual Ethics

1. Do not MAKE PROMISES!

There is a real temptation to promise something when you encounter poverty. "We will see you tomorrow," "We will be back again," "We will get it back to you." And we really do mean it. However, our situation may change, and we must remember that we cannot control what we will be assigned to do tomorrow! Neither can we make promises for our hosts to follow up on what we promised or would like to see them do. As you already know, unfulfilled promises hurt everyone's credibility.

Promises also can lead to dependency. Those you promised begin to "expect" what you promised rather than doing for themselves. You can say, "I hope we get to come back, but I can't promise."

2. Bring Self, Not Gifts

> Leader: Again, this section applies to everyone, even those only on day trips!

1. Due to customs regulations and because most hosts desire focus on RELATIONAL-based ministry, most countries do not accept gifts-in-kind.

We may bring supplies for our work which may include stickers, coloring books, etc. for children, or tools for building, medicines for clinics, etc. But look at this note from one of our hosts:

> We are all generous, well-meaning people who want to give from our resources to those who have less than we do. Done correctly, this is helpful. Done badly, it creates dependency, teaches others to be beggars, and causes jealousy between those who get something and those who don't.

2. Four Reasons Why Not – Remember the Four C's:

   a. Creates DEPENDENCY — We have to decide whether we are helping or enabling.

   b. Causes JEALOUSY — It may be hard for us to grasp how poor, and often starving people, get so jealous over the blessings of others. When a child sees someone else get something he/she perceives is prettier, better…children, even parents get hurt.

   c. Cost of CUSTOMS — The cost of customs is almost always exorbitantly expensive..

   d. Culminates in ETHICAL ISSUES — Are we being honest if we try to sneak something into a country when we know they require customs fees for the items?

BEFORE giving any monetary or other gifts, our leaders will check with our hosts.

We must remember that one of our goals is to assist our missionaries. If our hosts agree for us to bring gifts, they must be allowed to distribute them after we leave, not while we are there. They know who is the most needy and it gives them opportunity to be effective in ministry after we are gone.

LAB WORK

Scriptural Basis for Missions: In small groups, discuss the following Scriptures. Look at the texts from two sets of eyes:

1) How does this Scripture apply to me personally?
2) How do I see this Scripture applying to my involvement in an upcoming trip?

Share with each other. Select a group leader and share the highlights of your discussion with the class.

Philippians 2:1-11   Ezekiel 18:7   1 John 3:17-20

> Leader: 1) Do not feel that you have to use all the Scriptures
>   2) Feel free to select other appropriate Scriptures
>   3) Use as many of these lab assignments as time allows for your setting

Review RESURRECTION'S Trip Agreement – See Appendix 3

Reverse readings from previous lab session – Men read even numbers (2, 4, 6, 8, 10)
Ladies read odd numbers (1, 3, 5, 7, 9)

Practice Being A Witness Download and practice using 1Cross.com
— Practice w/Tracts
— Practice w/Bridge Illustration

Review RESURRECTION'S Agreement with Cooperating Agency – See Appendix 2

Practice Encouraging our Hosts

Discuss how to pray for our host missionaries

Evaluation Question: What was the most beneficial (new or best reminders) you received?
Answer: I liked the personal practice…I need more practice witnessing.

—Gennelle Conway
2017 Mission Training

HOMEWORK

Review chapter 4 – what were some of the highlights you want to remember?

Be sure you know our Church Vision, Purpose and Mission Statements (p. 8)

Read chapter 5
(Pencil in answers you anticipate)

Bring to Class Next Session: Bible and Pen
Personal Calendar
I-phone or Android with downloaded 1Cross app

Leader: Brainstorm briefly: What was the #1 take-away from Session 4?

SESSION 5

Devotional and Prayer

GETTING READY EMOTIONALLY

Preparing for the <u>HEART-MOVING</u> Experience

Learn the Culture

1. **Many times, there is a <u>CULTURE SHOCK</u>**

We minister to the poorest of the poor – tent cities, dirt floors, no running water or refrigeration, outdoor toilets; few are obese and few reach old age. Often, they are diseased, but don't know it, or believe they can do nothing about it. They may bathe and drink dirty water and seldom if ever see a doctor.

2. **Learn the <u>CULTURE</u>**

Use <u>YOUTUBE</u>. Look up the area where you will go. Familiar yourself with their work, history, politics, customs and laws. Learn and get mentally prepared and you will be more loving and understanding.

3. **Show respect even if you <u>MIGHT NOT AGREE WITH THEIR POLICIES OR VALUES</u>**

4. **Prepare yourself for a <u>HEART-WRENCHING</u> experience**

Don't ridicule, nor show pity. They are proud and do not want sympathy. Be humble and respectful. Remember God loves them every bit as much as He loves you!

Linda Mills delivering love gifts to Schertz Fire Dept.

Focus on <u>RELATIONSHIPS</u> Over <u>PROJECTS</u>

1. **Understanding cultures of most third world countries means understanding what <u>THEY VALUE</u>**

2. **Put <u>MINISTRY</u> and <u>RELATIONSHIPS</u> above <u>TASKS</u> or <u>GOALS</u>**

Quit work to talk with people! You can't spend all the time visiting, but minister to people!

3. **Be satisfied with <u>SMALL ACCOMPLISHMENTS!</u>**

Sitting with Honduran child, 2011

Sometimes miracles come in small packages! Someone well said: "I may not be able to do great things for the Lord, but I can do small things in great ways."

> The needs are so great that any little thing we do will be an improvement and we can never do enough.
> —Erskine Sealy
> 2014 Mission to Haiti

It is easy for a team to get caught up in the successful execution and completion of a project and fail to build good relationships with the people they came to serve. Leaving a project uncompleted can have rewards in itself! It gives the people in the area a work to complete for themselves, and a sense of dignity and reason to be proud. It gives the host missionary and other mission organizations an opportunity to continue working with the people.

> Evaluation Question: What was your best experience: Interacting with some of the children that I saw last year. It was rewarding to see some of the young men and they remembered our interaction.
> — Don Young
> 2014 Mission Trip to Haiti

4. Remember you are part of the BIG PUZZLE!

Your part is important, even necessary. The puzzle is not be complete without you. But you are not the LAST nor ONLY piece.

Engage people. Use LOCAL LEADERS to organize their people. Engage homeowners to help build their home, local people to organize for seeing doctors/nurses, church members to build their own church and community to dig their own water wells. Always expect more of yourself, but teaching is more important than doing the work yourself. Remember too: we have a lot to learn from them.

Special Note, If we come and have not learned something, we have missed our mission!!

Building church, Kenya, 2016

Preparing for the
UNEXPECTED Event

Elizabeth Elliott, whose first husband was killed in 1956 by Auca Indians in Ecuador (at the time unreached people group) said, "There is no faith without awareness of danger."

What can possibly go wrong?

Leaders: I like to brainstorm here and let your people answer –

Be ready

To SUBMIT   For SICKNESS

To SACRIFICE   For HOSTILITY

For ACCIDENTS   To GIVE your very life

Voodoo Flag, Haiti

Security – Guidelines for safety to keep in mind while on mission

Haiti Team Shirts, 2013

Two Philosophies: Leaders or group must decide which to follow

1. **WEAR UNIFORMS** to stand out!

Everyone will know us. Numbers scare thieves, vandals, gangs.

2. **BLEND** in with the people!

Blending with people, Haiti, 2013

Look-alike shirts might make us a target. Call no attention to team. Never say, "We are on a mission trip."

Regardless of the uniform, Stay in GROUPS – Never go off alone, there is safety in numbers

The fact is your leaders cannot protect you if you stray off alone.

Keep valuables locked up and OUT OF SIGHT – Vehicles, tools, materials

Be AWARE of your surroundings — Who watches, follows. whispers

Never bring VISITORS into living area! – obvious security risks! Remember those are not our homes. We ourselves are guests!

Evaluation Question: What was the most beneficial (new or best reminders)? Answer: Security warnings are important – good! The security video was very informative.

—Madeleine Roberts
2017 Mission Training

Friends coming to living quarters in Haiti, 2012

I cannot tell you how many people have asked, "Pastor, are we going somewhere safe? What can I say? Three crucial points to remember:

1. Our **GOD IS A GREAT GOD** who has gotten us through many tough times, and I have every confidence He will do so again – if that is His will.

Fact: The Lord may let us go through tough times to use us for His glory. I must go prepared to suffer if that is how the Lord will get glory. I tell my family and church, "if I die on the mission field, I will die serving Him and seeking to fulfill my mission. Bring my body back, celebrate my victory, but don't quit going!"

2. What if the **APOSTLE PAUL** had that philosophy – that we will only go where it is safe? We would not have half of our New Testament

3. The safest place to be is **WHERE GOD WANTS YOU** – quote from pastor friend, Jim Stephens, deceased when his daughter was a missionary in a dangerous part of the world

Prepare for **EMOTIONAL** Victory

Go HUMBLY submitting, but EXPECTANTLY, with CONFIDENCE in the Lord

One of our men made his first trip to Haiti in 2013. As we drove along the streets of a village, rocky, potholes, rough terrain, he said, "I thought, 'what are we doing here?'" When we finally pulled to a stop at a dirt-poor village, he said, "What in h…are we doing here?" Then he experienced servanthood. To my Friend's credit, at the end of the week, he said, "if you will give me an application for next year, I will sign it right now."

Go to WITNESS and MINISTER

Pic's with Joe Tex Band, Lake Providence, LA, 2012

- We are going not just to do good humanitarian work
- We are going to look for someone to share a WITNESS
- Keep your head up – Get in on what God's Doing

Remember stop the work — to WITNESS, minister
— or to MINISTER
— or ENCOURAGE someone

Be FLEXIBLE/FLUID

- Remember again: Your mission job may change from that which you have prepared for
- You may be asked to do a job and you may not understand why, it doesn't make sense.
- Sometimes you may need to walk away calm yourself, pray, trust the Lord!

So, there may be times that you may need to just calm yourself and pray with confidence that the Lord knows what is going on even if you don't. He sees the overall picture. So, we must trust Him in pressure moments to change or to work out the details or conditions we find ourselves in.

One of the mission organizations we have worked with has said it very effectively:

Be FLUID – We said (Session 2), "Be Flexible." Now rethink from flexible to FLUID. Water poured into a container, is flexible, taking the shape of the container. But spilled on a table, it's fluid, running as far as it can go. Situation determines shape. This is what we must do to be effective as servants.

Remember Who sent you and be available to Him through His choice of your leaders. Doing this, you will be able to see His hand in the most unexpected times and ways.

Final Challenge

Let's Get In On What God Is Doing...

A. This means change our thinking From <u>SELF-CENTEREDNESS</u> To <u>GOD-CENTEREDNESS</u>

It is easy to be God-centered Sunday, but Monday, Tuesday…How? Ask, "Lord, what do You want today?"

B. This means change our thinking From <u>LOCAL</u> To <u>GLOBAL</u>

It's not about us or our church, but Kingdom." If we will focus on building the kingdom God will build His church!

C. This means change our thinking From <u>TEMPORAL VALUES</u> To <u>ETERNAL VALUES</u>

Jesus: "lay up treasures for yourself in heaven, for where your treasure is there will your heart be also."

D. This means change our thinking From <u>SECURITY</u> To <u>SERVICE</u>

We take every safety precaution, but the Lord may want to use us in tough times to be His witness.

E. This means change our thinking From <u>COMFORT</u> To <u>SACRIFICE</u>

Servanthood is often uncomfortable. We might sleep on the floor. In Haiti, after the 2010 earthquake, many were lived in tent cities. I said, "If these people can live this way every day, I can do it for a week."

F. This means change our thinking From <u>BIG RESULTS</u> To <u>SMALL ACCOMPLISHMENTS</u>

First mission trip: seeing the multitudes I thought, "Lord, what can seven of us do?" He said, "One at a time."

Have a good Experience!
Someone has asked us to come. We go to share Christ and support our missionaries. Have a good experience. Remain safe and healthy. Plan, pray, prepare well. But God never fails!

What are the most important things you learned from these training sessions?

> Thank you for the opportunity…It was a life-changing trip and I think about what I learned almost daily. I have a renewed appreciation for what I have spiritually and materially. After Belize, I felt an intense need to…prepared for future trips...I don't know if I would have made this move forward prior to the trip.
>
> —Bettina McGriggler
>
> 2014 Mission Trip to Belize

> Evaluation Question: What can we do to improve?
>
> Answer: Keep doing the trips and we learn from experience what to do and what not to do
>
> —Karen Minor-Hudson
>
> 2014 Mission Trip to Haiti

Come Back Home To <u>SERVE</u>
One of our goals is to come back more faithful and better examples at home. Remember, you are a missionary at home as well as on the foreign field. The fields are white!

> Evaluation Question: What did we do well?
>
> Answer: providing the booklet/guide to this training. It was helpful in the classroom and to review as we prepare for missions
>
> —Lourita Schafer
> 2017 Mission Training

FINAL LAB

Scriptural Basis for Missions: In small groups…Scriptures. Look…two viewpoints:

John 6:27   James 2:14-17

1) How does this Scripture apply to me personally?
2) How do I see this Scripture applying to an upcoming trip?

Share with each other. Select a group leader and share the highlights of your discussion.

> Leader: 1) Do not feel that you have to use all the Scriptures
>   2) Feel free to select other appropriate Scriptures
>   3) Use as many of these lab assignments as time allows for your setting

Review Our Trip Agreement – Leader alternate with trainees, read every-other statement
Leader read odd numbers (1, 3, 5, 7, 9)
Everyone read together even numbers (2, 4, 6, 8, 10)

Practice Encouraging our Hosts – Discuss how to encourage our host missionaries

Please fill out the evaluation on the last page of appendix (Appendix 4)

Review Your Manual Periodically

Evaluation Question: Overall in what areas do we need to improve?
Answer: Sharing the Gospel needs to be focus at every session
—Karen Butler
2017 Mission Training

Evaluation Question: What was the most beneficial (new or best reminders)?
Answer: Enjoyed the Lab Work.
—Belinda Evans

Evaluation Question: What did we do well?
Answer: Everything, because I didn't realize how much the church as involved with missions
—Marie McGarity
2017 Mission Training

AFTER THE APPENDIX

For Leaders To Think About

Provide, Provide, Provide!

As stated, we must take our commission personally and seriously and we must change our mindset, or we will never accomplish our mission! Many boast of holding a service once a week in a nursing home. That's good but, how many people are actually involved? Only a few? What about the other 90%?

Many churches speak braggingly about their church going to Canada, China, India, or somewhere, even about having a mission to the local nursing home where they hold a service every week or month. I'm not knocking that. I pray we will keep that up. What I am asking is, "How many of our people are actually involved with us in those ministry efforts?" Most of time only a few are there to represent the whole church – maybe only 7-10 people. What about the other 90% or more of the church?

Encourage people to get out of their comfort zones and become servants. Challenge them. Break the Lord's Commission into four areas (Jerusalem, Judea…). How many potential service opportunities are in each area? Start with one. Put the word out. See who volunteers. Don't be discouraged if only one steps up. That is one more than you had before in a ministry you were not doing before. Fire spreads, but first, someone has to light the spark! Then ideas spark other ideas. As the servanthood ministry grows, you will find leaders in each area. Encourage, build them up, train and send them out!

As the servanthood ministry grows, you will find leaders in each area you go into. Encourage and build them up! Train and send them out! Watch, wonder and rejoice in seeing them grow into disciples!

We began to realize the Lord brought several nationalities to our membership – Haiti, Mexico, Africa… The Lord surely had a purpose for bringing them. If they would train, lead, and go on a mission trip to their homeland, we had on our rolls what we needed – translators, people who knew the culture, and knew where the need was. What a resource. So, we put the call out. Guess what! People signed up!

Acknowledge, Acknowledge, Acknowledge!

Phil. 2:3: *Let* nothing *be done* through selfish ambition or conceit, but in lowliness of mind let each esteem others better than himself.

Nothing motivates people more than being recognized. The most esteemed coaches are those who give credit to the team for victories and accept responsibility for defeats themselves.

What are some ways to acknowledge your best servants?

Two of the most effective tools I use:

1. Gifts/Awards: Recognize them in front of others with gifts and awards! This is a great way to pat them on the back and let them know how much you appreciate them.
2. Publish their pictures – Not only does this encourage those who participated, but it also might challenge others to believe that they can do this to get in on it the next trip.
3. Report – Give your faithful servants an opportunity to share their experiences

HOW TO TAKE PICTURES WHEN YOU CAN'T TAKE PICTURES

Sometimes picture taking is not advised without permission (Children's homes, museums, theaters, some government buildings...) Also, we never want to leave the impression that we want pictures to take back home and show how we came to work among the poor. Still, pictures are a valuable way of documenting work and if handled correctly, building relationships. Here are some guidelines:

A. Ask for permission – Most people would gladly allow their picture to be taken, especially if you have built a relationship with them. However, if they say, "No" then don't take their picture!

B. Take shots of your people working in the area, not of specific natives, children, or inhabitants.

C. Take shots of buildings, conditions, etc. rather than shots of the people

D. Take far away group shots so that you are not focusing on specific individuals

Plan for Overnight Travel

Prepare Ahead for Your Team

Appoint a Trip Leader to make arrangements for your team. The trip leader should keep Servanthood Pastor-Leader in the loop for approval.

Connect with a missionary, church or mission organization. Often, they will do preparation with you. If working with a missionary or church, you may need to make sure:

1) Meals are planned before your arrive. When and where will you eat? Will the food be sanitary for your team? Remember natives of other areas are used to eating the food in their area, but it may not be safe for your team. Be sure it is washed and cooked properly.
2) Plan well in advance for your travel. Will you need to make airline reservations? If so, contact the airline and ask if they will waive the baggage fee. Often airlines will give discounts or waive some baggage fees if you let them know you are going on a humanitarian service, particularly If there has been a recent disaster in the area.

If driving, obviously plan your route and do you need to secure drivers (bus, car, or van). Rent vehicles?

Don't forget to check what travel will be like in the area where you are going, and who will provide it?

3) Prepare for your accommodations. Where you are traveling, who and what kind of accommodations will be needed / provided? Does your team need to take bedding? Do you need battery operated fans? What should they expect?

Devotional Booklet

Devotional guides as preparation for a servanthood trip or service accomplishes several objectives

1. Encourages members to start a quiet time if they do not already have the practice in their lives.
2. Reminds servants that prayer and devotionals are a serious part of the work.
3. Helps keep focus on upcoming service, their own spirit, attitude and praying for the work.

Prayer and Fasting

Setting aside an agreed upon time, for prayer and fasting is a really effective tool for preparing teams.

1. Helps build camaraderie in the team as they get and focus together on their upcoming ministry.
2. Helps again reinforce the importance of prayer and personal spiritual preparation for a trip.

Watch Security Warnings

Our government's security warnings are helpful. As mentioned in training, we try to take every safety precaution. The last thing we need is negative publicity for having put our people's safety at risk. We want to go wherever the Lord leads and we are confident He will either protect us and bring us through, or use us if an unexpected danger occurs.

Remember: Romans 8:16-18 (NKJV): [16] The Spirit Himself bears witness with our spirit that we are children of God, [17] and if children, then heirs—heirs of God and joint heirs with Christ, if indeed we suffer with *Him,* **that we may also be glorified together.**

[18] For I consider that the sufferings of this present time are not worthy *to be compared* with the glory which shall be revealed in us.

Having said that, we are still called to be wise as serpents, and harmless as doves (Mt. 10:16).

Be aware of security warnings from our government and from missionary and mission organizations where you go to serve and cancel or postpone a trip if necessary.

Train, Train, Train

1. Review "How To Study and Teach This Manual" (before Table of Contents)
2. Provide constant and re-occurring training to recruit more servants and help servants keep charged and up to date.
3. Consider Hosting a Training Event (See Appendix 10)

APPENDIX

Appendix 1
Training Material Resources Come From the Following Contributors

Baptist General Convention of Texas Disaster Relief
Ben Freeman, Retired, Texas Baptist Men Disaster Relief
Bill Bright, Crusade For Christ
Cooperative Baptist Fellowship
Ed Sundman, lay mission leader, First Baptist Church, Universal City, Texas
Ernie Rice, We Care Haiti
Every Nation Ministries
Four Corners International Ministries
Marla Bearden, Baptist General Convention of Texas Disaster Recovery
Mercy International Ministries, Albuquerque, New Mexico
On Mission Magazine
Paul Powell, The Last Word, Copyright 2004 Paul W. Powell
Resurrection Baptist Church Next Step 401
Rick Warren, Saddleback Church, Huntington Beach, California
Southern Baptist Convention
Texas Baptist Men Disaster Relief
The Hole In Our Gospel, by Richard Stearns, 2009-2010 World Vision, Inc., Thomas Nelson Publ.
Timothy Phanner, lay leader, Vista Community Church, Temple, Texas
Together for Hope, Lake Providence, LA
Trinity Baptist Church, San Antonio, Texas

I want to thank and give acknowledgement to each and every one who has had a part in my training and education to become a servant. I have learned from you, even when it did not always look like it at the time. Your input and influence in my life and ministry is more valuable than I can possibly put into words.
Don Jeffreys

Appendix 2
RESURRECTION'S Trip Agreement

I ACCEPT THE FOLLOWING GUIDELINES FOR MINISTRY, TEAMWORK, AND SAFETY AS WE SERVE:

1. I understand that I am a guest, working at the invitation of a local missionary or pastor and that the people, pastor and missionaries will stay long after I leave.

2. I understand that I have come to learn and work alongside of people God loves in the community where I will be serving. I will strive to remember not to be exclusive in my relationships. If a sweetheart, spouse or my child is on the trip, I will make every effort to interact with all members of the team and those we work with, not just my family or best friends.

3. I understand that I may come across procedures that I may feel are inefficient or attitudes that I might find closed-minded. I will resist the temptation to inform our hosts about "how I do things." I will be open to learning other people's methods and ideas. I will respect the hosts knowledge, insights, and instructions.

4. I understand that part of the purpose of this trip is to witness and experience faith lived out in a different setting from what I am accustomed to. I will respect and show gratitude for the host's view of Christianity.

5. I understand that I am expected to maintain a servant's attitude toward all nationals, locals and my teammates.

6. I understand I must watch my speech and not gossip or slander anyone.

7. I understand that the work may become tiring or at times seem boring, but I will refrain from complaining. I know travel can present numerous and unexpected and undesired situations, but the rewards of conquering the circumstances are immeasurable. I will strive to be creative and supportive.

8. I understand political situations may be tense at any given time. I will refrain from negative political comments or hostile discussions.

9. I understand I must be mature and I will refrain from any activity that could be construed as a romantic interest toward a national or local citizen. I realize that many activities that may seem innocent in our culture may seem inappropriate to others.

10. I understand that my witness and lifestyle is the most important thing I bring. I will abstain from the consumption of alcoholic beverages and the use of tobacco or illegal drugs while on the trip.

Signature:_____ **Date:**_____

Please attach a copy of your passport to be kept on file in case of emergency

Passport Number_____ **Date of Expiration of Passport**_____

Appendix 3
Prayer Partners

_____   _____
Name of family prayer partner   Name of church member prayer partner

Prayer Partner's contact info: Phone, email, home address

_____   _____
Phone   Phone

_____   _____
Email address   Email address

_____   _____
Home address   Home address

_____   _____
City, State, Zip   City, State, Zip

Appendix 4
Evaluation of Class Mission Training

Name _____ (not required)

Note: Giving your name, you agree to allow us to publish your comments with your name in future publicity. Please give honest feedback. If we use negative comments, we will do so anonymously

What was the most beneficial (new or best reminders) from each session?

Session 1 —

Session 2 —

Session 3 —

Session 4 —

Session 5 —

Please answer as briefly as possible:

1. **What is one thing you should never say of a mission trip?**

2. **What is one thing you should never do on a mission trip?**

3. **What is one purpose you should always seek to accomplish on a mission trip?**

Overall what did we do well?

Overall in what areas do we need to improve?

Thank you for your response!

Appendix 5

Would You Consider Hosting A Training Event?

We want to visit with you
We will share how you can host at little or no cost and set up a schedule to fit your needs!

We would appreciate your contact information or: donjeffreys@yahoo.com 210/849-1746

Printed in the United States
By Bookmasters